TIBBETTS BROOK PARK, 1953

Lee Slonimsky

Spuyten Duyvil
New York City

Acknowledgements

I have in my eight previous collections acknowledged many crucial people who have continued to be important to my writing with their support, insight and feedback. Let me also mention others who have been particularly supportive recently: Dr. Robert Basner, Judy Carman, Rosemary Donnelly, Licia Hahn, the late William LaRiche, Stamatis Polenakis, Walter Preston, and Steve Ragno. Elizabeth J. Coleman provided a fantastically perceptive critical reading of the manuscript. Carol Goodman and Nora Slonimsky gave crucial "rankings" and commentary regarding particular sets of poems which were central to the manuscript.

Much gratitude to the editors of the following journals in which some poems first appeared, occasionally under different titles or in slightly different form: *Blueline* ("Hint"), *Green Hills Literary Lantern* ("85%", "Forever"), *The Homestead Review* ("King Geography", "Silver Water"), *The Lyric* ("Money Isn't Everything"), *Miller's Pond Poetry Magazine* ("Fox", "Tibbetts Brook Park, 1953"), *Muddy River Poetry Review* ("Crispness"), *The Night Visitors by Carol Goodman* ("Shining"), and *Trinacria* ("In Common").

© 2019 Lee Slonimsky

ISBN 978-1-949966-58-9

Library of Congress Cataloging-in-Publication Data

Names: Slonimsky, Lee, author.
Title: Tibbetts Brook Park, 1953 / Lee Slonimsky.
Description: New York City : Spuyten Duyvil, [2019] | Summary: "Poems in
    three sections: one memory of a visit to a park; two ruminations on
    Pythagoras's life and meaning; three enduring lifetimes"
Identifiers: LCCN 2019026145 | ISBN 9781949966589 (paperback)
Classification: LCC PS3619.L67 A6 2019 | DDC 811/.6--dc23
LC record available at https://lccn.loc.gov/2019026145

Lee Slonimsky's new collection contains numerous examples of formal poems that marry his remarkable ear for true verse and an almost genetic gift for mathematics; with rare intelligence he conducts novel explorations of Nature's miracles, flower petals arranged in prime numbers and the wondrous geometry of bird flight. Slonimsky begins with his earliest childhood memory of entering a re-imagined woodland and expands his naturalist's vision outward into the cosmos, evolution and paleontology; the book concludes with a new brace of poems about Pythagoras, his spiritual ancestor. Along the way Slonimsky meditates on bears and birds of prey, seasons and swallows, and gives us a remarkable series of poems about the dragonfly and the gnat. In a single altered sonnet we are introduced to "treemath," the legacy of Continental drift and the "shark's geometrical fin." His dragonflies, "those ancient mathematicians," "have parabolas/ in their potent blood." There is no one else writing about nature today who combines such close looking with almost mystical speculation and scientific data. Among many highlights, Slonimsky enacts a gentle political stance in "King Geography," writes "Shining," a wonderful triolet for his wife, and creates a poem of absolute magic and mystery, "The Living Dust," a masterful break dance into free verse.

    MICHAEL SALCMAN, M.D., EDITOR OF POETRY IN MEDICINE (PERSEA BOOKS, 2015) AND AUTHOR OF A PRAGUE SPRING, BEFORE & AFTER (2016), WINNER OF THE 2015 SINCLAIR POETRY PRIZE FROM EVENING STREET PRESS

Lee Slonimsky's latest collection of poems offers the reader a lifetime of accumulated wisdom through a series of gentle, profound meditations. This philosopher offers penetrating insights through simple, incisive words. His thoughts encompass the totality of time from the Big Bang to the perpetually elusive present second. Space is given comparable thought—ranging from the universe to the gnat ("...royal gnat... you're my hero... Your concentricities in air amaze.") All nature is respected. Observations concerning trees, dragon flies, birds and other companions found in our world are acknowledged and celebrated. These poems convey a reverence for all life.

    E. WARD SMITH, POETS HOUSE BOARD MEMBER.
        GROLIER CLUB POETRY EVENING HOST

For Ginger F. Zaimis,
Illumined Poet And Thinker

CONTENTS

INTRODUCTION by Sharon Israel   ix

PART ONE: CONCENTRICITIES

"Tibbetts Brook Park, 1953"	3
"Poet's Roulette: Winedark Sea"	5
"Craftsmanship"	6
"Do Trees Have Parents Like We Do?"	7
"As Faintly As a Brook"	8
"Still Free"	9
"Crispness"	10
"The Duel"	11
"Hint"	12
"The Note Pad"	13
"The Brrr Hour"	14
"The Bear of Bellows Lane"	15
"Silver Water"	16
"300 Million Years? A Drop in the Bucket Next to Sixteen Billion"	17
"Straight Dart"	18
"Shadow of the Dragonfly"	19
"Fakery Among the Ferns"	20
"Black Flower"	21
"Hints"	23
"A Place You Know"	24
"King Geography"	25
"Paleontologists Gather"	26
"Raptor Intercept"	27
"The Living Dust"	28
"85%"	29
"Concentricities"	30
"Dance"	31
"All in the Tiny"	32
"Neanderthal Burial Ground"	33

"No Place to Go"	34
"The Hangman Hangs"	35
"Above"	36
"Transmigration"	37
"Fox"	38
"Forever"	39
"Shining"	40
"Fore *Shadow* ing"	41
"Descartes, Who Called Animals 'Machines'"	42
"The Smell of Coffee"	43
"Money Isn't Everything"	44
"Dappled Breeze"	45
"Windless Simple Air"	46
"Arizona"	47
"The Winters of Our Years"	48
"Blue Wind"	49

PART TWO: THE LIMITS OF ENTITLEMENT, 525 B. C.

"Pythagoras's Peers"	53
"Pythagoras Counts"	54
"In Common"	55
"Pythagoras's Lament"	56
"Pythagoras Among Flowers"	57
"Uncertainty"	58
"A New Courtier, Crotone, 540 B. C."	59
"Pythagoras and the Queen, After the Courtier Departs"	60
"Kindness"	61
"Pythagoras in His Thoughts"	62
"Banking"	63
"Solitude"	64
"Xanthes and the Tyrant"	65
"The Limits of Entitlement, 525 B. C."	66

AFTERWORD by Barbara Ungar   67

Tibbetts Brook Park, 1953

Introduction
Sharon Israel

Lee Slonimsky, my first poetry teacher, my friend and my mentor, wears his enchantment with the workings of the universe like a second skin. I am always struck by how his unique version of the cosmos makes him hold deep bonds with dichotomy – with the past and the present, the animate and inanimate and stillness and movement.

Slonimsky has been my Virgil in exploring a larger world that features a vivid and sweeping commonality. He has also guided on-air listeners during his eleven appearances to date on my radio show *Planet Poet – Worlds in Space*. Slonimsky has an extraordinary ability to weave complex sentences and ideas into lyric simplicity, to effortlessly share the twists and turns of his lovely streams of consciousness.

During an expert and intimate on-air conversation centered on his collection *Pythagoras in Love*, Slonimsky worked his magic to coax listeners into believing that they too, like Pythagoras or Slonimsky himself for that matter, can transmute into a tree or a hawk, if only for the duration of the show.

In Slonimsky's newest collection, *Tibbetts Brook Park, 1953*, he poses a question in the title poem that startles and amuses with its audacity.

> Does light swim?

And gives an even more surprising reply

> The answer's in this little brook,
> sunlight striking, breaking up
> to motes of luminescence that
>
> do a fast crawl.

Here, Slonimsky erases the middleman of matter - he is friends with light itself, and engages in a kind of synchronized swim with its glowing specks, those "ancient primal swimmers that might as well have dived right off Big Bang." Slonimsky can relate:

> I too am spawn of Big Bang
> though rather latterly,
> as these early lightmote travelers
> startle me with just how they
> speed up when they swim
> across the sprawl of noon

In *Tibbetts Brook Park, 1953, Part One: Concentricities*, Slonimsky introduces a new take on how we experience matter and light – the concept of concentricity as it relates to inner and outer systems that reflect each other. Each system of concentric circles shares a common center. From this common center all things are held in echoing proximity.

I know this sounds too weighty to reach the heart, too good to be true, but Slonimsky does this with humor, lightness and language that sparks a feeling of play and joy:

> from singular origin
> one tiny seed
> the waybackwhen black ghost
>   "All in the Tiny"

There are many examples of circles surrounding a central core (the Big Bang, perhaps?) in Slonimsky's poems. Taken together they create lilting movement choreographed for the reader. For instance, in "Dance," his daughter twirls in ballerina class while black mini-flies whirl.

No one and nothing wants to stay put! In "Crispness," seasons venture out of their defined, separate rigor, one into the other, and seemingly with intent:

> The yellow leaf that falls in August
>
> shows
>
> the *annuality* of autumn; like
> a summer day in March.

Or, a creature with wings evolved 300 million years ago insists on dining on the surface of a "sparkling lake," intruding on a human sleeper ("Shadow of the Dragonfly"):

> he comes up on you unawares while you doze
> a visitor from the ancient past
> as modern as your blood.

And, in a signature move, Slonimsky tantalizes the reader with the possibility of trading places with those in different circles, exchanging one form of locomotion for another ("Transmigration"):

> *One species to the next: ten million years;*
> *and evolution can't be rushed.*
> *Transmigration is a much faster road:*
>
> you could wake up one bright morning soon
> and find yourself a gnat,

The poet keeps the reader moving – whirling, looping, flitting and darting along with each poem's protagonist. We even play roulette, that splendid embodiment of concentricity, "with shimmer, ripple, breeze" ("Poet's Roulette; Winedark Sea.")

Suddenly, in *Part Two: The Limits of Entitlement, 525 B.C.*, the reader finds herself in Crotone, southern Italy, where Pythagoras lived and worked almost 2500 years before the poet's 1953 swim in Tibbetts Brook. This abrupt switch to a firm time and place is almost like being in Dorothy's house as it hits the ground after the tornado stops spinning. In *Part I*, Slonimsky relentlessly shifted the reader from one end of time to the other, and now the reader feels a new relative stillness, a rooted present. 525 B.C. seems absolutely contemporary.

I'm totally there with Pythagoras as he contemplates the limits of his entitlement, as he grapples with his own mortality and failure, and with Xanthes, a fictional banker, whose "idol was Pythagoras" as he extols the virtues of kindness:

> Xanthes' idol was Pythagoras,
> the loving wizard of the abacus,
> who never hurt nor ate, an animal
>   "Kindness"

Yet, Slonimsky strongly tethers the reflective *Part Two* to *Part One*. Concentricity shows itself in the very structure of this book. The reader can look at both sections and experience them as two separate concentricities, or as concentric circles in the same system, revolving around a common center of history. *Part One*, later in time, might revolve around *Part Two*, the earlier world of Pythagoras and Crotone.

I am moved by the poignant connection between two brooks: the one that runs through Slonimsky's childhood and the one Pythagoras contemplates in Crotone. In "Pythagoras Counts," Slonimsky imagines the mathematician thinking as 'the brook runs bright in early morning sun."

He'd 'like to count the ripples up to one" but then resigns himself to his own imperfections and to the limitations of mathematics.

> A scholar all his life, he's finally learned
> that One's the only non-detail.

Slonimsky has created a marvelous journey, fulfilled his own "spin legacy" with truth and delight. Even the whorls of my own fingerprints affirm the life of these absurdly beautiful poems beyond the page and prove that perhaps the dance itself is the answer.

Part One:
Concentricities

Tibbetts Brook Park, 1953

Does light know how to swim?

The answer's in this little brook,
sunlight striking, breaking up
to motes of luminescence that

do a fast crawl.

They're ancient primal swimmers that
might as well have dived right off
Big Bang.

In the early 1950s
two grandmothers watched me swim
in the huge blue pool at
Tibbets Brook in Westchester,
the last I can recall
seeing either one of them.
Now that moment comes to life:

I gaze upon much *older* ancestors
from this wooden footbridge,
slivers of photonic streak
gliding on black water
fed by icy tributaries
in the sudden thaw of March.

I too am the spawn of Big Bang,
though rather latterly,
as these early lightmote travelers
startle me with just how they
speed up when they swim
across the sprawl of noon.

Elegant yet lithe,
microscopically bright,
they'd cross the English Channel
if given the chance.
Just like my grandmothers
made the Atlantic Crossing
to a New World where
their grandson took a swim;
and they basked in August sunshine,
one of those eternal moments
gone before you know it.

Their faces gleam in memory,
as bright as light motes swimming.

To see the ghost of Big Bang
all I need to do is lift
my gaze from this sparkling stream
and gaze out at the sky.

Our *present* in this universe
is made up of the past;
like this rippling, lightstrewn stream,
it all goes by so fast.

Poet's Roulette: Winedark Sea

The poet partners with these shadowy woods;
collaborates for inspiration. Finds
an image in the shifting deep green leaves;
in sunbright brook; in how one spider weaves
a gauzy maze in warm and so slow winds.

And if he finds no images, then broods
on how erratic his weak fortune is:

he plays roulette with shimmer, ripple, breeze

on such long strolls in search of Homer's sea:
adapting birdsong; looking for a phrase
inspired by branchcreak, trunkmoan, beebuzz.

Yet woods' *unexpected* makes this poet free
to soar like sax, *wordhop*, accompany
himself with leaves, the bass of an old oak tree.

Craftsmanship

The publisher of trees is WIND AND SEED (LTD),
their offices on a mountain summit. Mail
your humble manuscripts; await replies
beneath gust-clouded, gray November skies.

The days grow shorter; lingering leaves turn pale
or a wan scarlet. What a challenging road,
such authorship, nobility in words,
inventive metaphors that soar like birds.

You wait with patience for a slow response,
as autumn turns to winter.

                                   Scribble notes
on Kafka's, Hopkins' posthumous success
in case the answer's "no." Down at the pond,
ice creeps halfway, a single gray cloud floats
in sky of frigid blue. You wonder less
about fame's vagaries; instead reflect
on how to further practice your one craft.

Do Trees Have Parents Like We Do?

"*Sunslant*, thin piece of light. Grab while you can!
What *excite* life can offer."

                                    So my Mom,
a bigger oak, explained our woods to me:
at least this was her own keen strategy
in summer's seethe, and also autumn's gloom.

A full tree now, at last I understand
her parent-pretense. She was more a pal
than a June Cleaver sort: I came from a seed,
blown here on April's gusts, and should be pleased
to be the child of random skies, of lulls
each afternoon when seeds take hold, when light
will dim so slightly that its slant seems frail.

Then I must grasp, and heed my Mom's insight:

inheritance is such a potent tool.

As Faintly As A Brook

Tyrannosaurus Rex once lived near here,
according to your fossil map. These hills,
so soft, late April green, of course mislead
with bland serenity. And true, no fear
of speed, grand scythelike teeth, *gushblood* that spills
from victims large and small. Right now. But deeds
of savage lunge continue to occur
in raptor dives, and knives and guns, and worse.

Twelve years ago, a triple homicide
in these slow tranquil woods. Unsolved, you've read.

A billion years to learn, yet violence stirs:
no fossil, *that:* it drives a sleek black hearse
wherever chaos wants to go. You hear,
as faintly as a brook, T-Rex at war.

Still Free

    for Elizabeth J. Coleman

The sunlight brightens sky-approaching leaves,
but not trees' lower halves, still lost in gloom.
Be patient. Slowly, always, sunlight moves.
The sunlight brightens sky-approaching leaves.
What air is left, this tangled forest saves,
and still—a deer or two—are free to roam.
The sunlight brightens sky-approaching leaves,
but not trees' lower halves, still lost in gloom.

Crispness

The yellow leaf that falls in August

shows

the *annuality* of autumn; like
a summer day in March.

Let go
of calendar style crispness,
perfect math;

immerse in unexpected curlicues,
like lilies, wind tossed, on a frozen pond,
mysterious in origin and green
as tangled oak crowns in the heart of June.

The Duel

The deep red of leaves *trills* the air,
as if color were sound.

It's that fraught moment
in early November
when dusk silences even crows;

and you know there's no
escaping winter,

rapier—like branches soon to be bare,
swording a frigid wind.

Snow piled everywhere in the woods,
as if clouds have descended and frozen.

Hint

The long flat muddy stream speaks of the month:
July, *droughtish*; its torrid color, *seethe*;
as if the sun expresses sullen wrath.

But far along the brownish gleam, you see
a dance of dragonflies above a pond;
maybe they celebrate mortality,
so imminent.

                Wingflash will soon subside
to empty autumn quiet. Rain will mend
all cracks and gullies, where sunsear has dried
the summer-withered earth unbearably.

Flat muddy stream. Beyond, some dragonflies
excited by a gleaming, shrunken pond
where lilies wilt, as in all past Julys.

So suddenly, a meagre hint of wind.

The Note Pad

The hottest rain's in mid-July, these parts,
and that can be relaxing: sauna-sheets that gleam,
or steamy drizzle. *Woods to walk in, larks
that lilt the blurry air.* Woodpecker clang.

It's strolls like these provide recurring themes,
rainsoaked or dry. Treemath. How warblers sing;

and now a blackwinged beetle, drenched, alights
on writing pad, umbrella-dried. Crawl's pace,
northsouth on pristine blank, phenomenally slow.

Then somehow recognition stirs, delights:
its speed's the same as Continental Drift's
that led to Africa, Brazil moving apart. You sense
both motions to be quite the same. A rate
as primal as earthspin's:

                or your heartbeat's,

                or a shark's geometrical fin.

The Brrr Hour

All seasons lie, but some more cleverly:

it's hot today. October 1st. Clearly,
the summer's back, will last a while, but no!

Some leaves are red as sunset; dragonflies
long gone; earth tilts; soon forecasts speak of snow.

You sense a flatter sunslant; and can surmise
astronomy won't change.

      There's last July,
deep in the unfamiliar north; late night
brought winter from mild breezy day; a chill
so bleak you slept on embers.

      What a lie,
that winter came, yet one brrr hour can kill!

You woke to yellow dawn's familiar sight;
such color leaves, though, several weeks away.

Why seasons lie so much, you cannot say.

The Bear Of Bellows Lane

She has a limp, the neighbors say; a gait
as awkward as can be. I've never caught
a glimpse of her, not to this very day.
But every time I take a walk I wait,
right where the deep stream intersects with Bellows Lane.

She visits there to drink: *exciting sight,*
her bending down to lap the water up,
that clear flow washing brown rough stones to smooth,

in my imagination only, as I stroll.

And I have never seen her! What I watch
today, instead, is a gray swallow loop
from birch to oak and back. No bear can match
these glides. I need to find my truths
in what I see myself, not in some talk:
I only know the saga of each walk.

Silver Water

A dragonfly
first discovered
certain types of loops,
three hundred million years ago.

Flying over silver ponds
in those brief summer lifespans
they still explore today.

Their size has dwindled
oh so spectacularly
from eight foot wings
to several inches length,

wings that shimmer still
in the fading light of August
that turns silver water
to a kind of silk.

(Loops that bulge, and loops that narrow.)

These ancient mathematicians
have parabolas
in their potent blood.

300 Million Years?
A Drop In The Bucket Next To Sixteen Billion

The loops of love these dragonflies perform
mid June before they mate
amaze the pond and all its denizens:

bullfrogs and lilies, blackbirds, damselflies
and individual sun rays splashing down.

A naturalist observer pauses,
notebook in hand,
binoculars set aside:

"what a distance, glimmering wing
to my own five fingered hand"

He notes this thought and looks around,
listens for a signifying sound
that will explain time
immemorial.

The silence is like sizzling sun:

dragonflies loop around
this morning's sliver of endlessness
that soon will fade to afternoon.

Straight Dart

The more you study dragonflies, the less
you understand their perfect race with light:
the science fades; their flash and skim indict
much human vanity. You soon confess
to barely grasping how such glides evolved
from single cells.

     And human beings: proud
of this or that, the Pyramids, how loud
a synthesizer plays.

     The earth revolved
far longer round the sun to stir this flight
than to create the great ape from the mouse!

Pride *is* original sin: now hear it hiss
in grandiosity, war-rants' delight.

This shimmer-blur, straight dart's simplicity
perfects all surging life's complexity.

Shadow Of The Dragonfly

Flitting across a sparkling lake
he comes up on you unawares while you doze,
a visitor from the ancient past
as modern as your blood.

The whisper of wings startles you
and you glance up to see his shadow
merge with his body in silver descent,
as he spies some evening movement.

How startling a shadow with its hint of size,
and how aerodynamically perfect the wings
three hundred million years ago devised.
Dragonflies grander than eagles
once ruled the jetstreams of swamps
and dodged meandering methane
with light quick curls of antennae.

Now greatly retreated in size
in a daily shrinking world,
dragonfly darts away from the water
to savor his evening meal,
shadow vanishing into rocks
as last waves of crimson sunlight
roll on toward the dusk.

Fakery Among The Ferns

The art of counterfeiting goes beyond
the human world: all mockingbirds steal sound,
and thieves among the humble ferns abound.

Not quite a modest million years ago,
a brand new species showed up here and there,
but after careful study it appeared
that it was more a replica. (The years
between its advents well beyond our minds
except for time's first principle: be slow.)

No hurry, never anyplace to go.

I love the way this sunset counterfeits
the light of sunrise, rose, three wisps of fleece;
my own blood thieves sea water. Pulse insists
on echoing the tides, yet more intense.

Black Flower

It strikes you right away when glancing down
at several purple rows of chicories:

the universe can count!

Where else did petal numbers come from?
(Seventeen or eighteen, twenty-one;
erratic but specific, mostly prime.)

The thrust to number in
a universal mind
is unmistakeable.

Counting atoms in our blood, the stars,
this browned-down autumn leaf descending,
all beyond our flesh capacities,
but parallel to petal counts
with shining chicories:

Atoms in each strand of hair,
a lofty oak, an asteroid:
these massive numbers *are* creation;
mysteriously
the universe can count!

This much was clear
to Pythagoras
and to ancestor hominids
well before
whose Achulean axe improvements
mandated TWO (sides).

They lived with starry, vivid skies
whose stars were like white, yellow petals
of a vast black flower;
their minds absorbed the math—nature
of creation,
and evolved to us.

(I shed the form of formal poet
and identify
with random, ceaseless math.)

Profound equations with a single goal:

complexity!

Hints

A hundred million years ago, this was
a jungle: see that flower, there. Yellow
despite December. And hear an insect's buzz.
A hundred million years ago, this *was;*
such signs persist in early morning haze,
and warmish winds, southwest, that start to blow.
A hundred million years ago, this was
a jungle: see that flower there. Yellow.

A Place You Know

This chicory was born to perfect math:
prime number petals. Seventeen. Nineteen. Purple.

You bend to gaze, the air so beautifully still
it's *immanent* along your high ridge path.
You breathe as deeply as your lungs allow
air's pure elixir; blue benevolence
infusing blood with seventh, eighth, ninth sense
of otherworldliness. A place you know.

Tranquility is frail, of course, and then
a sudden gust rips petals off. No proof
of math in tatter: only eight are left,
the judgement of a ruthless fleeting wind.
That other world is gone; *this* one remains:
mysterious, one which no math explains.

King Geography

The mathematics of bird calls astounds:

some patterns as precise as DNA,
while others fluctuate. But hearing sounds
seems such a soft and kind *identity*,

compared to our rude nationalistic ways:
our flags and guns. Our cold geography.

Paleontologists Gather

A fossil footprint stills the flight of time.

This tiny claw-like limestone imprint tells
of dainty pre-bird's gait. And triumph fills
the air as we all gather round, observe.

(Around that time there came a skeletal swerve
toward hollow bones and flight: true fossil fame.)

But daintiness deceives; such talons were
the deadly logic finishing all soar,
prey-spy, descent. Quick early mammals rent
in two by nails of plummet: we descend
from just such victims. Several of us wince,
as gazing brings forth reveries. Pursuit—
escape—print cannot give a hint;
but passing time itself's a solemn truth.

Raptor Intercept

Humidity stains fossil fragments gray
from faint dull white of bone: you too are blurred
by weather, tedium. This bird was mired
in mud some eighty million years ago;
you must keep chipping!

                               Revelation's slow,
but soon enough you'll see what time will say
about the bird, its origin, demise.

You picture it in flight: it soars above
Cretaceous jungle glistening with fog…
Why did it plummet, end up in a bog,
an ancient casualty to its surprise,
stuck motionless?

                       You can't let one fate *prove*
that bad luck always waits. You wipe your brow;
you wish a dry and chilly wind might blow.

The Living Dust

I was walking in the park when I found
a cantaloupe sized rock looking like
a dinosaur egg, fossil hard.
I took it home,
put it down,
went in another room.
When I returned the egg was hatching
or at least was breaking apart.
Within was a bird—
shell-breaking beak tougher than stone,
body green leather,
feathers black razors—
eyes full of blood.
It moved a wing
        hopped a step
                suddenly crumbled to dust.
I stared at fragments of shell
slicing the silent air
and breathed the living dust.

85%

You didn't *mean* to slap, but there she lies, inert:
your tiny colleague in the art of life.

Gnat, whose inner life's a mystery
except for thoughts like "sun" and "hover,"
"fly."

The instant that it took to smash her
could well have been much better spent
on simply breathing.

Blood, a tiny speck, glints now,
85% the same as yours;

as sun begins its afternoon decline.

Concentricities

You see the world through eyes so tiny that
a leaf's an ocean; or, at least, a lake.

You are Sir Wing Flash, flitting, royal gnat
and likely you will never write a book
or draw a sketch, or sing except for buzz,
but you're my hero, nonetheless.

                                          A breeze,
a gust, and now your whirl is gone; replaced
by empty sunlight. Here, amidst birch trees,
I ponder your quick-winged, spin legacy;
fine master of blue air, big crowd, flight pace.

I have a sense you know geometry!

Your concentricities in air amaze.

Dance

My daughter twirls at ballerina class
and when we step outside at 6 PM,
red sun on cobblestones (quaint parking lot),
black mini-flies are whirling in the dance
of insect love for spring.

My daughter's tired, needs to be carried
to the car.

But dark flies stay ebullient in the glow
of April's late day shimmer.

Whirl's their ritual.

All In The Tiny

The chaos and flutter of all the world's whirl
diverts me not at all

from singular origin,
one tiny seed,
the waybackwhen black ghost
of the cosmos.

I take my instructions in math
from prime-number-petaled chicory,
counting the leaves on a random tree,
and seeing the All in the tiny.

Neanderthal Burial Ground

At first the thinking was,
they'd left some flowers too,
because of so much pollen in the cave,

still measurable
after thirty thousand years.

But then the thinking changed.

Bees had brought the pollen
sometime later on.

Touchingly sensitive bees,
just as aware of death perhaps
as elephants with their graveyards,
lamenting another species passing,
as so many species could.

Bees' flowers crumbled long ago
but human bones remained,
not quite our own subspecies perhaps
but human enough, for sure.

A marker of their lives
lit by sunlight flooding this cave
since time immemorial,

even as we their descendants
shepherd bees all over the globe
toward extinction.

No Place To Go

> NY Times article 1/24/17: "some Neanderthal DNA
> can increase the risk for depression ... it all depends
> on where on the genome it's located"

I feel Neanderthal
sadness all this morning,
and not just due to ancient physiology.

I'm looking at sheer absence on my walk,
storm-sky intimidated birds and animals,
fled to shelter everywhere.

Just as *we* fled those final times across the Pyrenees,
then south to caves along the shimmering sea
where *we* ran out of time
and luck.

What contemplation silence now allows:

like asteroids remembering their long vanished planet,

or flutter-arcs of rising, mournful crows.

So long ago, *we* had no place to go.

"The Hangman Hangs" In Norwegian

"Dragningen Mot Dypet"

"Dragonflies must die" erroneously translates
the title of my wife's last book.

Perhaps they "must," but not likely! They've lived
fantastic epochs: think about the dates.
A hundred million years, they had survived
before *first* dinosaurs. What would it take
for them to vanish now? The planet earth,
imploding?

        They might even then persist; *glide—flit*
amidst some tattered tufts of air, their craft
of wing outwitting doom; a real rebirth
amidst earth's shattered orbit.

            As their wings
once spanned eleven feet, we humans rule
right now, but *they* must live or we will fall,
more fools of history. *The hangman hangs.*

Above

Josephus mentions that the Pharisees
were interested in *Transmigration*.

                          Now,
the graceful bound of this young deer reminds
you of an athlete: lofted, like a breeze,
above a rough stone wall. Does fate allow
for deer with human ancestors?

                          Behind
lithe deer, three more. No doubt, a hawk's blue soar
is *further* from we flightless humans, but...

Pythagoras amidst *The Jewish War*
still startles somehow; such an awkward fit:
Greek science and the Hebrew faith.

                          As if
they're distant cousins; *both in you*. You'd love
a future as a deer (despite no proof).

The hawk still circles toward the sun above.

Transmigration

A gnat that hovers
right nearby your eye
affords the opportunity to spy,
observe, track closely, *see*

this eagle turned quite miniature,
this pilot of the spare, blue-moleculed air.

And if you are so fortunate to hear
the infinitesimal buzz of lithe sweet wings,
you feel a surge of freedom deep within:

as if you're just about to grow the same!

Queen Gnat may rule a quite small space of air,
but in it gossamer wings have no peer:
your shoulder blades, where wings begin to stir,
must percolate with envy:
flesh, calm down!

One species to the next: ten million years;
and evolution can't be rushed.
Transmigration is a much faster road:

you could wake up one bright morning soon
and find yourself a gnat,

hovering with a buzz
in sunsmeared clearing in the woods,
no memory of your previous life
but sheer delight, in coasting smooth green air.

Fox

It's a beautifully still morning,
the only stirring
the cries of four different birds.

Blue sky so bright
any shard of it's a sapphire.

If winter days were always like this,
no-one would need the spring!

But then a single snowflake spins down
out of empty bright blue,
and you become as alert as a fox.
Even boulders seem to quiver
with a sense of the unexpected.
One bird departs, diagonaling
between tree tops and a scimitar
of pale midmorning moon.

The sun remains implacable
in its love for still-running streams,
and seeds in the ground.
Where black water crosses into open light,
sparkles are denser than any blizzard
March might surprise
these almost budding woods with.

Forever

The lit window:

it can mean *everything*,

on an otherwise dark street,
slit by the pale bone light
of a scimitar moon.

Your heart scurries
like a mouse in the shadows
at the thought of going home here
after so long,

and yet, the evening shortens;
an owl leaps across the moon.

Then inner excitement sounds like thunder
over the cement tundra.
Your heart cannot restrain itself:
you open the door to the stairs
above which a light bulb burns,

and you lean into always.

SHINING
(TRIOLET FOR THE NIGHT VISITORS BY CAROL GOODMAN)

A name can change one's core identity:
"The Furies" thus became "The Kindly Ones,"
Athena ending senseless cruelty.

A name can change one's core identity.

Benevolence diverts from treachery;
and, shining like her crown, pure goodness wins.

A name can change one's core identity:
"The Furies" thus became "The Kindly Ones."

Fore *Shadow* Ing

He struggles restlessly, deep in the night,
with something that he saw that afternoon:
the sharp etched shadows of oak leaves upon
the road, so sharp they briefly fooled his sight:

perceiving gray leaves of a flat gray tree.

As if idea and green flesh were the same;
as if intuiting some Plato dream
now lost in mist in a vague century
the future holds. *Which more real, he couldn't say*:

the sunwashed leaves themselves, or shadows' mime;
the signature of absent light or gleam
of sun on Maybalm leaves that tangle, sway.

Some might critique his thoughts as mystical,
but he deemed images the actual.

Descartes, Who Called Animals "Machines"

You'd like to sense a consciousness behind
soft rain in woods,
tree-pensive mood,
this Wednesday afternoon.

A deity for ants and moss,
a light when sun's not here.

You'd feel much less alone.

But mind *is* you
(blood splashed; astute)
however, and

the flitting bird, the flashing lizard both
are colleagues in pure mindfulness,
no matter what the party of Descartes might say.

When bee thinks flower,
moss soft rain,
they're just as smart as you.

Leaves are as certain truth
as all philosophy:
they think in green, always.

The Smell Of Coffee

If Paris wasn't here we'd have to try
inventing someplace similar; at least
a street like *this*: cafes, aromas, gleam,
an atmosphere that makes despair a lie.

But here we are; it's real, and so we feast
on bread and cheese, café au lait. The theme
of this slow hazy morning is our past,
as recent as it's distant when we speak
of this or that, Montmartre, Vietnam;
the way we'd planned to call the Left Bank home.

Like steam in chilly air, most plans don't last,
but fragrance can persist, just like the look
between us now, a two way mirror deep
with long gone shimmer. Brightening time's dark loop.

Money Isn't Everything

This is a rougher side street than the slick,
half atmospheric ones in the brochures.
Some cafes boarded up; some with a look
of dealers congregating; sordid wares
beyond our means or leanings.

                              Still, it's Paris. *Back
together now*, three decades passed: our love
transcends hard times, drab baggage, pain. The lack
of elegance in circumstance.

                              Above,
some wheeling pigeons gray the air, subdued
in grimly colored feathers; wine so cheap
it falls well short of water.

                              But our mood
makes air champagne: we toast our fate, and leap
from memories to prospects, new and fresh;

amidst our kiss this alley shimmers, lush.

Dappled Breeze

Sunglitter, windpuffed,
paints this ancient tree,

the one that half a millennia ago
had a real personality.

Now it sleeps so much and slouches
toward the shadows that arrive
as early as high noon.

Sunglitter moves across rough bark
as if its touch makes bark ridges tremble,

the dappled breeze of sunrayed love
relentlessly fond of the endlessly gaunt

tree,

lazing in the shadows.

Windless Simple Air

Listen to the silence of falling snow
until it pitter-patters on
branches, needles, frozen ground.

But silent through the air.

Then thin and reedy,
one dawn distant voice

pipes.

Flautist in the snow,
melodious and well-pitched,
blue if sound were color;

you can only picture
how this winged Beethoven
warbles in pure solitude
two or three woods away.

An audience of snowflakes
white-mirrors all the shimmer
of notes floating through air,

windless simple air,
that nourishes the woods
with blue transformed to whitish gray,
all snowy day.

Arizona

These branches and these bones are sunbleached white,
a white quite otherworldly.

                          Centuries
have slipped past since the massacre; the trees
gave bones, just like the Smiths did. Much gunfire:
it severed slender branches, limbs. Bloodbright,
the sun that set that day.

                          And now a choir
of desert birds laments yet flutes the past,
an hour before the newest setting sun
spills red across the mountains to the west.

Archaic, killing for religion, yet
it still goes on, this greatest earthly sin:
believing that your faith's the only one.

One pine still stands *here*…one lark settles *there*,
at rest from flight without apparent care.

Winters Of Our Years

Eight decades in the Catskills take a toll:

Jack Clegg grew up near Prattsville, never left;
he farmed his fifty acres till one fall
the bank reclaimed: he saw that more as theft
but shrugged, moved on. The Huntersfield Preserve
was not policed—subsistence more than farm—
but he was fine; he certainly saw no harm
in living off the wilderness. The curve
life threw him next was slowing up. Old age,
and this or that; arthritis; quick fatigue.

He wrote down this one line: "time is a plague."

Tranquility receded, turned mirage,
but the view from HF's summit stayed immense,
and spring would start, and life again make sense.

Blue Wind

Accounting's been Pete's life; now he's retired
and finds himself on morning walks immersed
in counting leaves. As if he's long rehearsed
for *this*: to be a naturalist who loves
the meaning of the smallest numbers; proves
an ant can add by watching. Long desired:
this forest for a desk. Swallow colleagues
who've mastered angles tax forms don't include;
frogs' pond leaps that raise up his studious moods.

(They don't teach nature-math in colleges.)

The nation's taxes are an artifice,
but *here* he feels at one with origin:
with blue wind, lush grass, butterflies and sun.
The math of flower petals. Green's pure source.

Part Two:
The Limits Of Entitlement, 525 B. C.

Pythagoras's Peers

In Egypt he had been *initiate*
in temple mathematics cult. Arcane,
their mysteries, but one (an architect
told him about), the "3-4-5," made plain
procedures for surveying.

                                            When he went
back home he made a reference to it; soon
he was acclaimed for *thinking;* took part in
his own great legend; grand embellishment.

For what is human nature but to love
sheer adulation, "immortality."

His peers, the gulls above, then tried to prove
their genius at a winged geometry,
a "3-4-5" of soar, a pattern to

remember, always: how these smart gulls flew.

Pythagoras Counts

The brook runs bright in early morning sun:
blue *waver* where large, rough stones lie below,
but otherwise an even, tranquil flow.

He'd like to add the ripples up to One,
as with the petals of a chicory,
whose seventeen or twelve wild nature made;

all count's a detail, tangible but crude;
their essence, One, proclaiming harmony
between pure math and his, a bird's, a stream's.

A scholar all his life, he's finally learned
that One's the only non-detail. Truth's turned
into this single word! Blue water gleams
in ceaseless race; its murmur reassures.
Here *One*, he sees, and tinkle, wash he hears.

In Common

So fascinated by the math of birds—
their sequenced calls, parabolas of flight—
that he counts much the day, then watches curves
of perfect winged design, in fading light.

Convinced these are his peers, he longs for some
discussion of joint principles: why three
recurs the most in patterns. Why the sum
of one bird's notes is different from the next.

But silences greets his warbles; so remote
the language-links that there can never be
the clear speech of a lecture in these woods,

or musical analysis. Just breath
intaken sharply at the width and breadth
of beauty's movement: how a math-bird *flutes*!

Pythagoras's Lament

The flutter of a butterfly demands
exotic math to fully comprehend;
and he is lost; his efforts do not end,
and something's always missing.

                                              Grains of sand
are easier to count. No rationale
for white-winged chaos can be found:
the lurch and drift, soft float, mislead his mind
in curlicues. He grapples now with *fail*.

All limits are more tangible with age,
and he needs to respect such boundaries—
it doesn't matter that he *was* a sage—

his grasp's confined to vague simplicities,
and even worse, his focus can be brief,
full in the grip of time, that hawklike thief.

Pythagoras Among Flowers

Their competition to attract, late spring,
the largest and most lustrous butterflies,
perhaps includes a strand of math.

                                          Obscure,
however; baffling him. Do petals bring
attention to themselves with patterns, size?
Or is it all quaint chaos everywhere?

He watches bright wings flutter—red, white, gold—
the flowers even more diverse, turquoise
and orange, pink.

                        Perhaps they see themselves
in flower color, petals stretched with poise
toward windy sky, small garden-flames-that-thrive:

some sort of cousins.

                            Tintage can't grow old
except it does (sudden-September), while…

all underlying math's immortal. *Friend.*

Uncertainty

Pythagoras has made a date
to meet his former Stoic rival, talk
about events of long ago.
Two men, one woman: hurts still linger, stalk
their chance encounters in the street.

"Let's clear the air."

He's early, now. A crow
is nibbling at some crumbs nearby;
no-one else is here; he's ready to wait
an hour or so. *The man's a fiend*
to not show up, (their rendezvous a lie),
but no, he'll come…in all this heat…

And sure enough, around a sunsoaked bend
in hilly lane, he now appears.

Like hurt from long ago: the sunlight sears.

A New Courtier, Crotone, 540 B. C.

A flatterer extraordinaire, he works
long hours to be stationed near the Queen;
and then the compliments, admiring looks
begin. A handshake lingers.

                                    Not quite a scene;
his timing is too sharp for endless stares.

The King's detached…and privacy's in vogue
at court; locked doors; yet vague suspicions nag.
Pythagoras sees both upon some stairs,
too close; hands locked. How could they dare?…

The King's his friend, as well as royalty;
he will say something. Let the scoundrel flee
before the squalor of adultery
spreads further…

Pythagoras And The Queen,
After The Courtier Departs

The Queen's subdued for days, then weeks. On walks,
she scarcely notices her favorite trees,
shrubs, flowers; sunlight on the pond. A breeze,
so warmly soft, is wasted on her frown.

King's summoned him to walk with her. P talks
of how his own awareness, now, has grown,
of math among the birds. Of trees' delight
in varying slants of light at different hours:
Crotone's woods, his tutor. She's enjoyed
such scientific monologues before,
but not today. Cold gaze. *The King's employed
him to divert, but no.*

                      A wan noon light
sifts through the royal, convoluted woods;
he lapses into sudden silence. Soon,
they're colleagues of a sort. How both can brood.

Kindness

Xanthes' idol was Pythagoras,
the loving wizard of the abacus,
who never hurt, nor ate, an animal.

X wonders now if change might help his health:
new discipline of eating only plants,
(less likely than the lambs to have a soul).

Crisp air, brisk walks, a swim: these are true wealth;
not jewels in their cases, endless land.

Xanthes had once met him, long ago;
a tiny child, he'd reached up for his hand
inside Crotone's court. The sage was slow
but X remembers a strong grip; the glow
in dark brown eyes. "A king without a crown,"
his father told him, afterwards. And now,
he craves the magic of that wizard's wand,
his meatless purity, transcendent mind.

His kindness is the perfect way to go.

Pythagoras In His Thoughts

Xanthes loves the morning like a friend;
the slope below his house so bright with sun,
his gaze must settle elsewhere:

                               on the clouds
that shade the streets of Athens. *Now*'s the time
last dreams distract from sorrow; he's serene,
almost, in day's first flush.

                       And if he broods
it's not on grief, but on the latest trend
in sculpture, verse; or how to find the sum
of all a forest's leaves and birds' deft notes
(a challenge that Pythagoras would love:
a theorem that could take ten years to prove.)

Distraction, that's the key. A long cloud floats
up toward him from the city; watch it close,
he thinks: so calm. The beauty buries loss.

Banking

Xanthes' patience has expired with
the endless doctors trekking up his hill
to minister to his fatigue, and aches.

The early morning breezes better soothe
his inflammations than their herbs: they're fakes!
His only remedy is force of will.

And then there is his pool, midafternoon,
the water's sunray-ribbed bright shimmer; warmth
suffusing his cold bones.

                            Athens, below,
distracting him. He's calm yet wishes so
for youth's return; he's found out life's a loan,
the interest payment rising every month.

Not wealth nor medicine can cure his drear;

his view this afternoon is all too clear.

Solitude

Xanthes keeps one bedroom empty. Gone,
his son, forever from a tyrant's war.
The furnishings the same as on the day
he left.

        It's suffering alone that won,
despite the fool's wild claims: he'd say
near anything to raise a cheer. Before
his twisted reign calm peace prevailed. But now
threats rattle the serenest moment. Light
replaces his boy's sleeping form: white glow
from a three quarter moon, that slowly flows
across the bed. Xanthes sits, reflects
on how his heart once leapt at the mere sight
of Diones, returning home. Respect
and honor, love, all crushed by tyrant's might.

Xanthes And The Tyrant

The view's so splendid from his balcony:
the Parthenon's grand columns, distant woods;

so steep the hillside where he's built his home,
he sees for many *stadia*. Sits, broods
on how his inner bleak geometry
contrasts with breathless sights. Though thoughts may roam
to this and that distraction they come back
to how he's lost his son to senseless war,
deep scars from such deranged cold tyranny.

The fleeting, bitter conflict was no more
than blood-soaked exercise in vanity.

He'd slit his throat himself, but he's too weak;
and so his thoughts turn toward conspiracy.

There's strength in numbers; justice won through blood.

The Limits Of Entitlement, 525 B.C.

Our neighbors kept a lion as a pet:

in stone walled, thatch roofed, strong enclosure but
sometimes they took the King for a long walk;
then everyone would hide inside. Rope-leashed
but there could be, just once…

                                        Above a hawk
would slowly glide, stare down, as if it wished
for just one chance to prove itself supreme
of all the beasts, with one unerring dive,
then *talons*…but that plummet never came.

The King intimidates! A hawk might prove
equations with sharp-angled flight, or kill
a feeble deer, if starving: *lion, no!*

And nervous we remained: whose blood might spill?

The real King wouldn't hear our pleas, and so
we gave up all our hawk hopes; one sad day,
we left our privileged street and moved away.

REFLECTIONS
ON *TIBBETT'S BROOK PARK, 1953*
BARBARA UNGAR

Lee Slonimsky is a walking poet. Like Mary Oliver, Thoreau, and Wordsworth, Slonimsky makes a daily practice of writing while walking. He is a saunterer, in Thoreau's punning sense in his essay "Walking": a "Saint Terre-er," one who walks (or saunters) toward the Holy Land. Thoreau claims, "An absolutely new prospect is a great happiness, and I can still get this any afternoon," by walking in a circle of a ten miles' radius. This image of a circle described by the radii of afternoon walks is an apt image for Slonimsky's poetry, fittingly geometrical to suit his alter ego Pythagoras: setting out from the same radiant center, always arriving somewhere new, each poem adventures into the unknown. In "The Note Pad," Slonimsky writes, "strolls like these provide recurring themes," and in "The Bear of Bellows Lane," "I only know the saga of each walk." This daily practice may account in part for his prolificness.

In this, his ninth, collection, Slonimsky plays variations on many of his favorite themes, in his favorite forms—sonnet and triolet, as well as free verse—moving from the recent past (1953 and forward) to the ancient past, 525 BCE, and further back to the Big Bang. His wide-ranging mind loves to travel, through time as well as space, musing upon mathematics everywhere. In the title poem that opens the collection, "Tibbetts Brook Park, 1953," he links his two grandmothers to swimming light that carries him back to "Big Bang," seeing its "ghost" in the sky, as he sees his grandmothers' ghosts gleaming in memory. Similarly, in "Do Trees Have Parents like We Do?" he compares his mother to an oak, himself to a seed. Themes of time-travel and cosmic unity lead naturally to metempsychosis.

Transmigration appears as one of the tenets of Slonimsky's Pythagoras, and as a rich vein for his own poetic speculation. In "300

Million Years?" his naturalist observes a dragonfly and wonders, "what a distance, glimmering wing/ to my own five-fingered hand." Several poems concern dragonflies, their looping flights a figure for the poet's own loops between the prehistoric past, when dragonflies had 8-foot wingspans, and the diminished present. Another familiar insect, the gnat, "your tiny colleague in the art of life," ("85%") inspires several poems and the idea of "Concentricities," which I take to be something like Dickinson's idea of Circumference. He imagines reincarnating as a gnat, a deer, an oak. He imaginatively inhabits each of these and many other forms.

In these sympathetic identifications with animals, insects, and trees, he also resembles Pythagoras, arguing against Descartes and company, most explicitly in "Descartes, Who Called Animals 'Machines.'" Here he admits, "mind IS you," but in Slonimsky's definition of "mind":

"When bee thinks flower, moss soft rain, they're just as smart as you. Leaves are as certain truth as all philosophy: they think in green, always."

Slonimsky thinks in green, always. In his poetry he performs what he variously calls "treemath," "nature-math," or the "math of flower petals. Green's pure source."

From such philosophical nature poems, he segues through a few more personal sonnets to his wife of many years, before looping back through the millennia to inhabit Pythagoras again, and a new character, Xanthes, an imaginary disciple of the philosopher. This second part, "The Limits of Entitlement, 525 B.C.E.," is more engaged with the human and political. Half a dozen or so poems are seen through the perspective of the aging Pythagoras, before switching to his new persona, Xanthes, who met Pythagoras once, when Xanthes was a child. Another half dozen poems from the perspective of Xanthes, now aging himself and in poor health, mourn the loss of his son in a pointless war, which he blames on an unnamed Tyrant. It is clear that Slonimsky's solutions to our recurrent human dilemmas would be those of Pythagoras: "His kindness is the perfect way to go," as Xanthes concludes in the poem "Kindness." Kindness, nature, and mathematics. And daily walks. Lots of walking. And poetry. Another link to Pythagoras in Slonimsky's work is that he reaches back to when poetry and music were one, when astronomy was listening to the music of the spheres. A common misconception is that poetry is somehow divorced from (if not opposed to) science and mathematics. Slonimsky rejects this false dilemma. One of the hallmarks of his verse is his ability to unite fields of discourse that are commonly kept in their own silos. A polymath who loves mathematics, science, and history as well as poetry, he makes all central to his poetics. He reminds us that "numbers" used to refer commonly to poetic metrics, at which he excels. His work recalls that of the ancient Greeks in healing this supposed rift between the humanities and sciences, by reuniting what has been cut asunder. He is always finding the one in the many, or the Blakean "All in the Tiny," as one poem is called. He keeps sauntering toward the Holy Land (his Holy Land, however, predates Christianity, mingling "Greek science and the Hebrew faith," as he notes in "Above"), discovering mathematical unity underlying the cosmos. Reading his work feels like drinking from a clear stream, or swimming in Walden Pond: one feels purified afterwards.

The Japanese term, *shinrin-yoku*, or forest bathing, acknowledges the cleansing and healing power of walking in the woods. Recent biometric studies have demonstrated that the vast preponderance of life on earth is comprised of trees: Slonimsky's mathematically attuned mind seems to have intuited this long ago, for he writes of trees and other plant-life as near and dear relations. From his first book, *Talk Between Leaf and Skin,* Lee Slonimsky has been writing of our kinship with trees, in a conversation that has only deepened with each successive volume. If you are not lucky enough to be able to go outside and walk in the woods yourself every day, keep this book nearby. You can dip into it at will, and feel some of the benefits of taking a walk in the woods, with an erudite and convivial companion.

LEE SLONIMSKY has published nine collections of poetry. His third book, *Pythagoras in Love*, has been translated into French by the poet Elizabeth J. Coleman, and is currently being translated into modern Greek by the poet Stamatis Polenakis. With his wife, Hammett and Mary Higgins Clark Award winning novelist Carol Goodman, Lee has co-authored the *Black Swan Rising* trilogy. Lee is also a hedge fund manager who invests on behalf of the welfare and humane treatment of animals.

www.ingramcontent.com/pod-product-compliance
Lightning Source LLC
Chambersburg PA
CBHW020145130526
44591CB00030B/229